W9-ACT-038

BABY ANIMALS

BABY TIGERS

by K.C. Kelley

AMICUS

paws

stripes

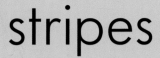

Look for these
words and pictures
as you read.

tail

whiskers

What is that?
It's a baby tiger!

Tigers live in Asia.
Baby tigers are called cubs.

See the tiger's stripes?
Their fur is black,
orange, and white.
Stripes help them hide!

stripes

Look at its paws.
Each front paw
has five claws.
Baby tigers climb well.

paws

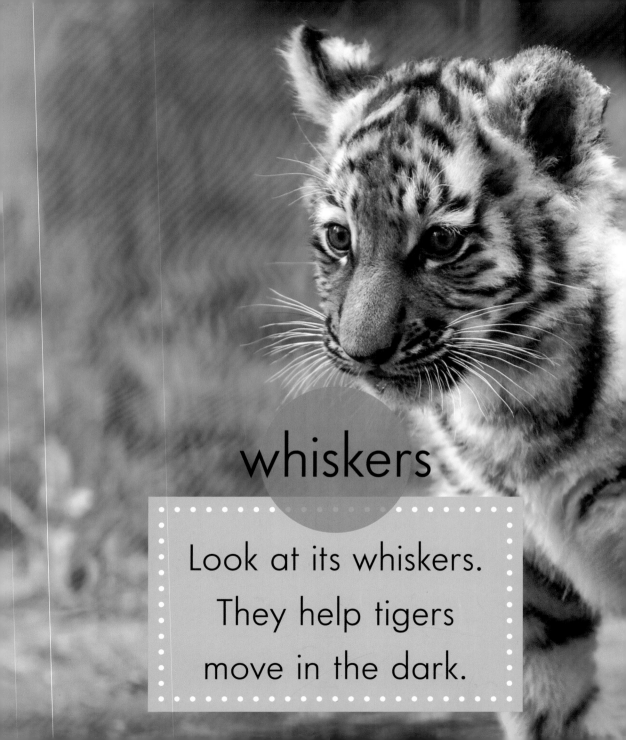

whiskers

Look at its whiskers.
They help tigers
move in the dark.

tail

See its tail?
Tiger cubs love to play.
One chases the other's tail!

Cubs hunt with their mothers.
Time to eat!

Look at its paws.
Each front paw
has five claws.
Baby tigers climb well.

paws

paws

See the tiger's stripes?
Their fur is black,
orange, and white.
Stripes help them hide!

stripes

stripes

Did you find?

tail

whiskers

tail

See its tail?
Tiger cubs love to play.
One chases the other's tail!

whiskers

Look at its whiskers.
They help tigers
move in the dark.

spot

Amicus Readers and Amicus Ink are imprints of Amicus
P.O. Box 1329, Mankato, MN 56002
www.amicuspublishing.us

Library of Congress Cataloging-in-Publication Data

Names: Kelley, K. C., author.
Title: Baby tigers / by K.C. Kelley.
Description: Mankato, MN : Amicus, [2018] | Series: Spot.
   Baby animals
Identifiers: LCCN 2017022574 (print) | LCCN 2017034356
   (ebook) | ISBN 9781681513379 (pdf) | ISBN 9781681513232
   (library binding : alk. paper) | ISBN 9781681522579 (pbk. :
   alk. paper)
Subjects: LCSH: Tiger cubs--Juvenile literature.
Classification: LCC QL737.C23 (ebook) | LCC QL737.C23
   K4575 2018 (print) | DDC 599.75613/92--dc23
LC record available at https://lccn.loc.gov/2017022574

Printed in China

HC 10 9 8 7 6 5 4 3 2 1
PB 10 9 8 7 6 5 4 3 2 1

Megan Peterson, editor
Deb Miner, series designer
Patty Kelley, book designer
Producer/Photo Research:
Shoreline Publishing Group LLC

Photos:
Cover: Isselee/Dreamstime.com.
Inside: Dreamstime.com: Anankkml
1, Rattanphoto 2tl, Andrey
Gudkov 2tr, Dr. Pramod Bansode
2bl, Stef Bennett 2br, Vikas Garg
3, Isselee 6, Julian W. 8, Vladimir
Cech 10. Minden Pictures: Suzi
Eszterhas 12, 14.

BABY TIGERS